Build a 1000 Gallon Aquarium

L. Lee Watkins

ISBN: 1502924498
ISBN-13: 978-1502924490

Any similarity to a sane person found in this book is unintentional and should be disregarded!

DEDICATION

I dedicate this book to my mentor, Wade 'Dub' Staats, who hired me to work in his tropical fish room when I was 13 years old. Dub also assisted me in my successful pursuit of an Amateur Radio License at age 14, which led to a degree in Electrical Engineering and a 44 year career specializing in Communications Systems.
Dub was a good friend and I miss him.

ACKNOWLEDGMENTS

I am forever grateful to Ellen, my wife of 53 years, who has tolerated my many hobbies, including my sporadic tropical fish obsessions.

INTRODUCTION

I was first exposed to the tropical fish hobby when I was thirteen years old. A neighbor who bred angel fish and other varieties for the local market hired me to work in his fish house.

During my teen years, I had a ten gallon community tank and a two gallon breeder tank in my bedroom. In the spring, I bred Zebra Danios, raised the fry in an outdoor pool (made from a baby bathtub) and sold them for ten cents each. Not much profit but great satisfaction.

In the 1960's I lived with my wife and two kids in Melbourne, Florida, and had aquariums all over the house, including a 55 gallon sitting beside the TV on a homemade stand in our family room. Three 20 gallon tanks were on shelves below. I also had a bedroom dedicated to breeding angel fish.

In the early 1970s we moved into a condo in Ft. Lauderdale, Florida, where I built a 160 gallon freshwater planted tank into the living room wall (a room-wide closet on the other side of the wall). I used fiberglass-lined plywood with marine epoxy paint. Eventually we sold the condo and the tank had to go; a sad day.

From that time until I retired in 2006, I had an urge to build a really big aquarium, and finally I did. When I designed our retirement home, I included a den with a 15 foot wide wall and a 9 foot high ceiling suitable for a large homebuilt aquarium. The final design produced the 1000 gallon monster described in this book.

I would not expect many people to duplicate this aquarium (you would have to be certifiably insane), but perhaps this book might inspire a few other aquarists to build the tank of their dreams, whatever size it might be.

THE FINISHED 1000 GALLON AQUARIUM (2010)

MY HOBBY/TV ROOM (2013)

- *My HDTV is in the corner left of the aquarium.*
- *My amateur radio station (W8SMF) and my computer are on the desk to the right.*
- *I do allow my wife to come in to check her emails!*

AQUARIUM DESCRIPTION

- Interior Dimensions: 10' long, 4.5' wide 3' deep
- Each glass is 2'x4' panel minus the seal area
- A partition divides the tank for different fish
- The aquarium is highly automated and monitored: Lights, water change, water level, heating, cooling, and feeding *when activated,* plus 32 status and alarm lights.
- The Control Panel is in far corner; the electronic chassis is in the cabinet below.
- For viewing from the outside, a CCTV camera is placed in front of the tank and the image appears on a monitor outside. The CCTV camera is shown on the white pedestal near the control panel
- The automated water change system includes a 300 gal/day RO system (Kent Liquid R/O Right is added for balance). A Total Dissolved Solids meter is used to monitor the water conditions
- The black front is vinyl sheet painted black.
- Frame is Red Oak with polyurethane coating
- The small door above the tank is the feeding door

GETTING STARTED

The walls in and out were finished using plywood siding, which is easy to remove and to saw. This wall has a header that supports the roof so studs can be removed.

THE FLOOR JOISTS

The wall studs are removed and the floor joists installed. The reinforced concrete floor is 8” thick. The weight of the finished tank will be about 8000 pounds.

THE INSULATED FLOOR

1/4" Plywood was fastened to the bottom side of the floor, then 6" thick insulation installed.

FLOOR INSTALLED

3/4" Plywood floor installed with brass screws.

FRONT ASSEMBLY (MUST BE VERY RIGID)

This assembly will be the front of the aquarium where the glass will be mounted. (2x12 frame with ¾" plywood face). Note doubling of ¾" plywood at bottom to support one end of a 45 degree wedge.

BLOCK AND TACKLE TO RAISE/LOWER THE FRAME.

FRONT ASSEMBLY FIT CHECK

The front is on place temporarily. Note the cutouts for the glass and the 45 degree wedge at the bottom. The wedge prevents a blind spot due to the floor of the aquarium being a foot below the glass. The front cutouts were marked at this time.

POSITIONING THE 10' X 20' RUBBER

This rubber was heavy. I used a cart to get it from my trailer to the site, and I rigged a block and tackle to lift it to the platform.

LINER READY TO INSTALL IN THE FRAME

The pond liner is heavy and unwieldy. Would have been good to have had help!

SEALING THE GLASS TO THE RUBBER LINER

The First Compression layer is shown. Glass and rubber is sandwiched between the front plywood and the oak strips and secured with brass wood screws. No glass installed at this stage.

TWO COMPRESSION SEALS

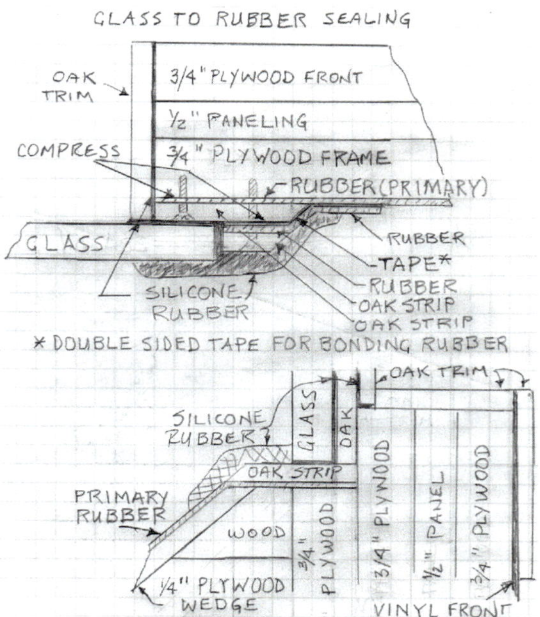

CUTOUTS IN THE WALL

FRONT ASSEMBLY IN PLACE

The PVC pipe in lower corner is a conduit to the far side.

BUILDING THE 2X6 FRAMING

FRAMING AND ¾" PLYWOOD LINING IN PLACE

The plywood interior was sanded smooth and painted with two coats of enamel paint.

INITIAL POND LINER INSTALLATION

POND LINER WITH CORNERS FOLDED (TRICKY!)

Felt material sold by the manufacturer (Firestone) was placed on the floor under the rubber.

BUILDING THE HINGED COVER (2X10 BOARDS)

COVER WITH WINCH AND SAFETY LINES

At this stage I was using a hand-cranked winch with a high gear ratio.

BUILDING SIDE WALLS

TOP AND SIDEWALLS FINISHED

The interior walls and the top are covered by vinyl sheets for water proofing. All hardware is brass or stainless steel.

SPLIT LIGHT TRAY FIT CHECK

Glass panels in the bottom will pass light and prevent water from entering from below. Four two-bulb 40 watt florescent reflectors will be mounted in the top. The two power strips are for the 'low light' period and the 'high light' period. The A/C will be removed and a larger swing out door will be installed.

TOP PART OF LIGHT TRAYS WITH FIXTURES

BOTTOM PART OF LIGHT TRAYS WITH GLASS

The eight fixtures support 16 each 40 watt bulbs. Later, four of the fixtures were modified to accept compact florescent. Cabinet latches release the two halves. A 3X pulley system is used to raise/lower the light trays.

HINGED ROLL OUT FILTER PLATFORMS

TOP OF LIGHT TRAY IS VINYL OVER ¼" PLYWOOD

Note the two muffin fans that cool the light tray (air pulled through the two holes in the near corners)

FILTER/HEATER ASSEMBLIES IN PLACE

Two Ocean Clear Canister Filters and two 300 watt in-line heaters on each side. Later, I found that one 300 watt heater was enough. Each filter operates with 600 gallon/hour water flow. The light trays are raised and lowered by the compound pulley systems shown.

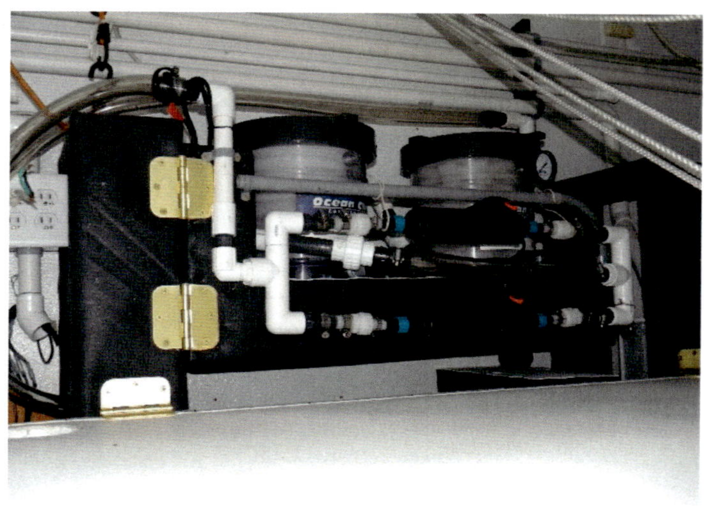

HOMEMADE PLANTERS

Above: The triangular planters fit into the shelf cavities (back six) or sit on the floor (front three). The three studs shown in the planters have hooks for lifting. A pulley system mounted on the underside of the cover is used to install and remove the planters.

Below: Foam shelves to be covered with rubber. A 'hot-wire' cutter used to cut foam.

THE PLANTER SYSTEM INSTALLED

The back set of planters is elevated ten inches by two foam slabs. The foam is prevented from floating by the vertical wedges on each back corner and by a 2"x2" aluminum angle that fits across the full width of the aquarium on the front edge of the top foam.

The wedge on the left houses a Rio HF20 1200 gal/hour submerged pump and a pre-filter inside a 6" PVC pipe.

The intake for the filter pump is at the front left bottom corner covered by a mesh screen. An identical wedge/pump assembly is located on the right side.

The center wedge houses water level sensors in a four inch PVC pipe and a drain pump in another four inch PVC Pipe (part of the automated water change system). Note the black rock that fills the blind spot in the front left corner. There is a similar rock wedge in the middle blind spot and the other front corner blind spot.

THE CONTROL PANEL AND RELAY CHASSIS

The top section of the control panel is the aquarium controller. A nine zone lawn sprinkler controller is used for timing. The switches on the left select manual or automatic control of the lights, heaters, water pump, air pump for the left side of the aquarium. The switches on the right perform the same functions for the right side.

The bottom switch on the left controls the automated water change system (manual or automatic operation). The bottom switch on the right controls the alarm system (local-off-remote).

The center section has 32 LED indicators for alarms and status. The bottom section is my lawn system controller (not related to the aquarium).

The Control Unit uses relays to control the various functions. The chassis is located in the cabinet below the Control Panel. Wiring from the Control Unit passes through the wall to the Junction Box on the outside wall.

EXTERIOR VIEW OF THE LEFT REAR

Sink on the left; storage cabinet, 300 Gallon/day Reverse Osmosis System (Part of automated water change system); Junction Box. The ½" PVC pipe around the edge of the aquarium is the overflow tube (alarmed).

FINISHED EXTERIOR WITH HINGED STEP-UPS OPEN

The open door on the right side is the exhaust port for the thermostat controlled circulation fan. The intake is located on the far side of the hood. The fan assembly consists of four high-capacity 115 VAC muffin fans.

It turns out that the circulation fans maintain 78 degree water temperature without the air conditioner throughout the Florida summer months. Between the lights during the day and the in-line heaters at night, the water temperature is very stable during the Florida winter months.

Note the access panels in the walls for trouble shooting. Also, the panels on the back access the air pumps and terminal strips (part of the control system).

Note the two fold-down shelves on the back wall. These shelves are used to hold Vortex diatom filters for cleaning the water after a major internal disturbance (for example, removing and replacing a planter).

BEFORE THE SCREEN INSTALLED

AFTER THE SCREEN INSTALLED

I now have a 115 VAC power winch on the cover. The manual winch outside is backup for the power winch.

From the first photo showing the opening of the wall to this photo spanned a period of 4 years!

OPEN HOUSE FOR SHOW AND TELL

Viewing a Slide Show on Computer

Giving the construction and operation spiel
(When their eyes glass over, quit talking!)

Viewing the front/interior of the Aquarium

THE MOST RECENT PHOTOS - 10/23/2014

Photo from left half of aquarium – Angels and compatibles

Photo from right half of aquarium
Community emphasizing Tiger Barbs and Neons

Algae is controlled by proper lighting plus one Common Pleco on each side. Common Plecos are traded/replaced every 6 months or so because they get very big very fast.

Photo of angel pair in left half of aquarium

This pair of angels fish spawns regularly, but the eggs do not survive predators. Kribensis spawn and raise young.

UPKEEP AND MAINTENANCE

I clean the filter pads, trim the Giant Val and clean the light tray glass every 10-14 days (the glass is only two inches from the water, so algae grows on the glass). I have two sets of filter pads, so I can wash the dirty pads after completing the change-out.

I have a quart-size bag of charcoal in one filter on each side. I change out the charcoal and clean the pump pre-filter every other time.

The water quality and interior of the aquarium are essentially maintenance free (except plants).

During the three years the aquarium has been up and running I have replaced the Rio HF20 pump on each side one time within the last six months. They do run 24/7, so no surprise there.

I replace all florescent lights yearly (staggered)

I have pulled one planter (a front corner) to replant.

I have had one overflow alarm, but that was due to a freaky event. A PVC elbow sprung a leak and squirted water directly into to the overflow pipe opening—one chance in a million, but it happened.

There have been no problems with the control system.

SIMPLIFIED CONTROL SYSTEM SCHEMATIC

This page shows the Time Controller, the Automated Water Control and the Light Control

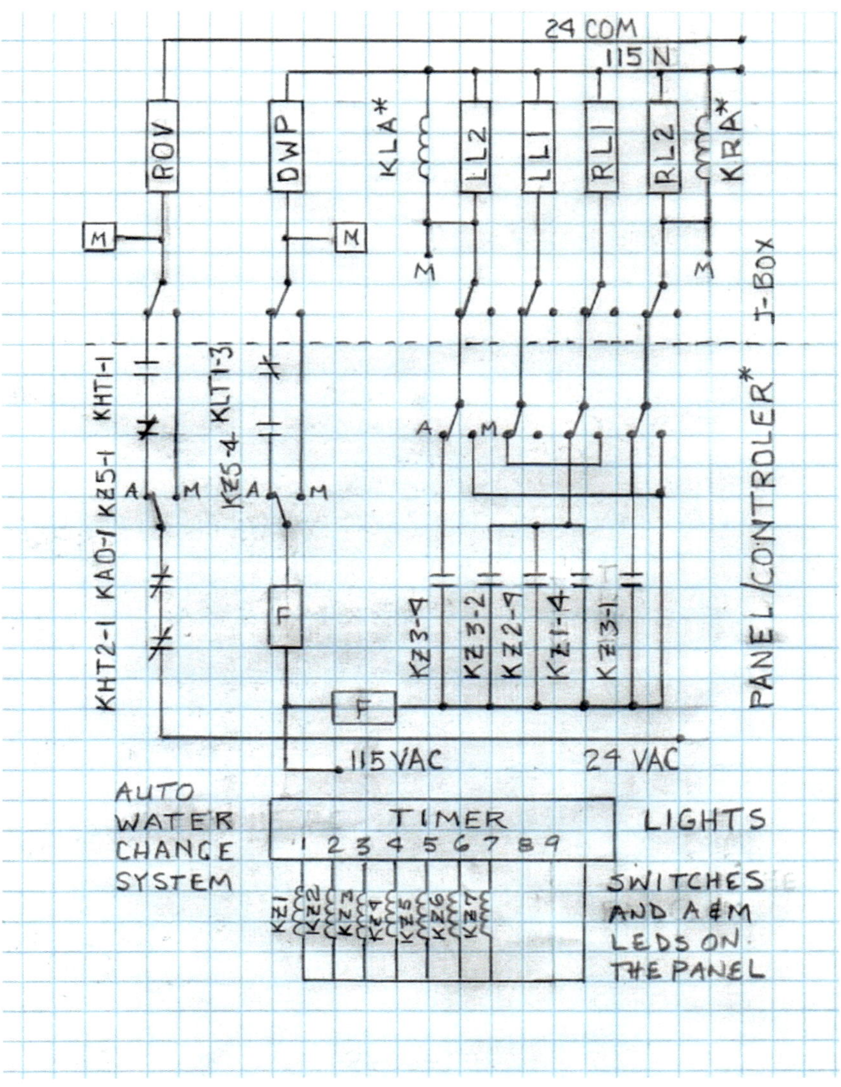

SIMPLIFIED CONTROL SYSTEM SCHEMATIC

This page shows the left side Water Pump/Filter Control and Alarm and Monitoring

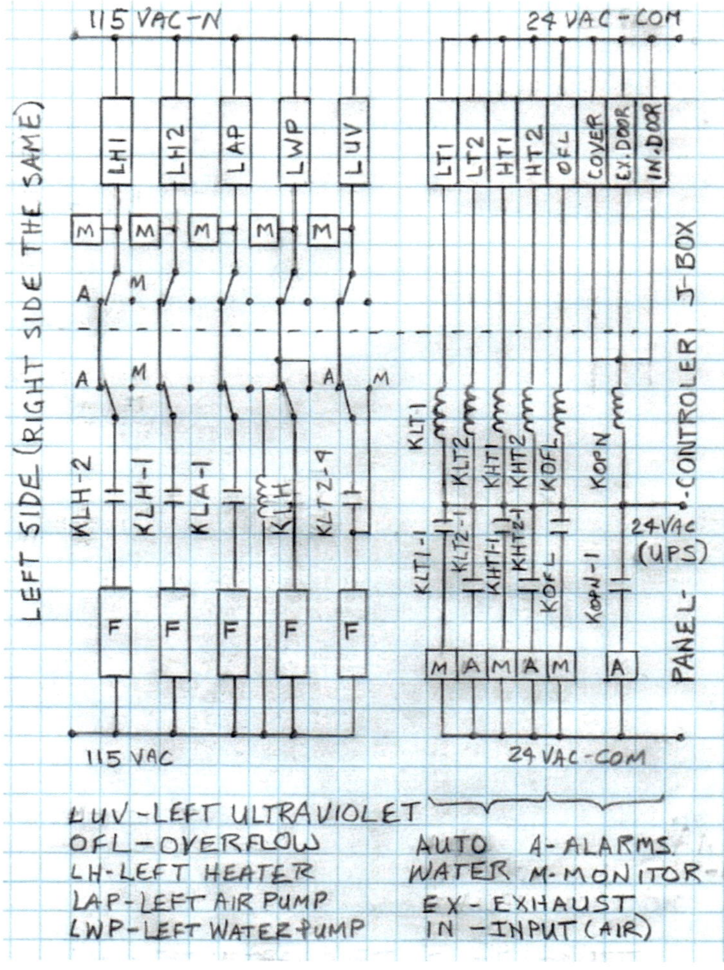

SIMPLIFIED AUTOMATED CONTROL OPERATION

The schematic diagrams above show the basic operational subsystems of the automated aquarium. The descriptions below follow the diagrams.

Timer: Because most of the timed control functions are relatively simple, a standard sprinkling system controller was used (Rainbird SST-900i). This type of 'zone' controller has a four hour maximum zone-on time. Because lighting control was more complex, I had to use the *multiple times per day* function.

Light Control: At 8:00 AM, Zone 1 comes on, energizing relay KZ1 (a 4 pole relay). KZ1-4 turns on the low lights, a low light wakeup call for the aquarium. At 9:00 AM, Zone 3 comes on energizing KZ3 KZ3-1, 2 and 4 which turns on the full lighting. AT 12:00 PM, Zone 2 comes on, energizes KZ2 which turns on the low lights for an hour. At 1:00 PM, Zone 3 comes on for three hours. At 4:00PM, Zone 2 comes on again for one hour. At 5:00 PM, Zone 3 comes on for three hours. At 8:00 PM Zone 2 comes on for one hour. At 9:00 PM lights are off.

Water Pump Control: The filter system pumps run 24/7, but precautions are taken to turn off the in-line heaters when water flow is interrupted. If power is applied to the pumps (LWP and RWP), KLH is energized and KLH-1/2 and KRH-1/2 keep the heaters on. If power to either pump is lost, power to LH1, LH2 and/or RH1, RH2 is turned off. The heaters do have an internal thermostat, but I did not want to take chances with a 300 watt device.

SIMPLIFIED AUTOMATED CONTROL OPERATION

Air Pump Control: When the lights are on, KLA and KRA are energized and the air pumps are off. When the lights are out, the air pumps come on via KLA-1 and LRA-1.

Automated Water Change System: The water level sensors are magnetic switches made of a fixed shaft and a cylindrical float that moves up and down the shaft. KLT is set for Normally Closed and KHT is set for Normally Open.

When Zone 5 comes on, KZ5 energizes, KZ5-4 closes and the drain water pump (DWP) is powered via KLT1-3. At the same time KZ5-1 opens preventing the reverse osmosis system (ROV) from coming on. When the water level goes down a little, KHT1-1 closes but has no effect because KZ5-1 is open.

When the water level goes down to the preset depth, LT1 opens and turns DWP off. After a few minutes, Zone 5 times out, KZ5-4 and ROV comes on. When the water level is at full depth, KHT1-1 opens and ROV turns off. Note that relays KAO-1 (Overflow Alarm) and KHT2-1 (backup high water sensor) function as fail-safes.

If water level goes down due to evaporation, HT1 closes, KHT1-1 closes and water is added until HT1 opens again. The sensors operate with about ¼” level

change.

AQUARIUM WITH ISOLATION TANKS IN PLACE

- The tanks on the right are 10 standard
- The tank on the left is a 20 long
- Isolation tanks are removed when not in use.

If you enjoyed this book, please write a review on Amazon.com

Also check out novels written by L. Lee Watkins

The Dallas Kincade Mystery Series

The Key West Caper (Book 1-2014)
The Ballroom Boondoggle (Book 2-2014)
The Sugarland Surprise (Book 3-2015)

The God Ship Science Fiction Series

The God Ship (Book1-2014)
The Cloud People (Book 2-2015)
The Flyers of Volca (Book 3-2016)

For Information on L. Lee Watkins go to
http://www.lleewatkinsinfo.com

- Science Fiction and Mystery Novels
- W8SMF Amateur Radio Information
- 1000 Gallon Aquarium updates
- Ballroom Dance Activity

A HUSBAND-WIFE HOBBY – DANCESPORT
Competition Ballroom Dancing (retired)

- USA Dance* Senior (Over 50) Open American Smooth National Champions
- Seven times finalists in USA Dance Senior Open International Standard
- Two-time finalists in Senior North American International Standard Championships
- Winners of many Regional American Smooth and International Standard Championships

* USADance.org (Amateur Ballroom Web Site)

Made in the USA
Middletown, DE
12 November 2024